I COME TO SERVE

By Edward M. Grosz

I Come To Serve

A Guide for
Special Ministers of the Eucharist

Pueblo Publishing Company

New York

Nihil Obstat: Robert E. Zapfel
              Censor Librorum

Imprimatur: Edward D. Head, D.D.
              Bishop of Buffalo

March 4, 1987

Design: Frank Kacmarcik

Excerpts from the English translation of Holy Communion and Worship of the Eucharist outside Mass © 1974, International Committee on English in the Liturgy, Inc. All rights reserved.

Scripture texts used in this work are taken from the New American Bible With Revised New Testament, © 1970, 1986, Confraternity of Christian Doctrine. All rights reserved.

Copyright © 1987 Pueblo Publishing Company, Inc.
All rights reserved.

ISBN 0-916134-87-3

Printed in the United States of America

PREFACE OF DEDICATION

Love is lived and learned
and shared
because it becomes incarnate
in the mystery of each person.

I wish to dedicate this work
to two special persons,
my mother and father,
Helen and Joseph Grosz,
whose love has given me life,
and inspired me
to love others into life,
that Life,
who is Jesus,
the Bread of Life!

Contents

CHAPTER ONE 9
One Who Serves

CHAPTER TWO 13
Becoming Like Christ

CHAPTER THREE 25
Ongoing Study and Renewal

CHAPTER FOUR 29
Attitudes and Demeanor

CHAPTER FIVE 43
Extension of the Special Ministry of Holy Communion

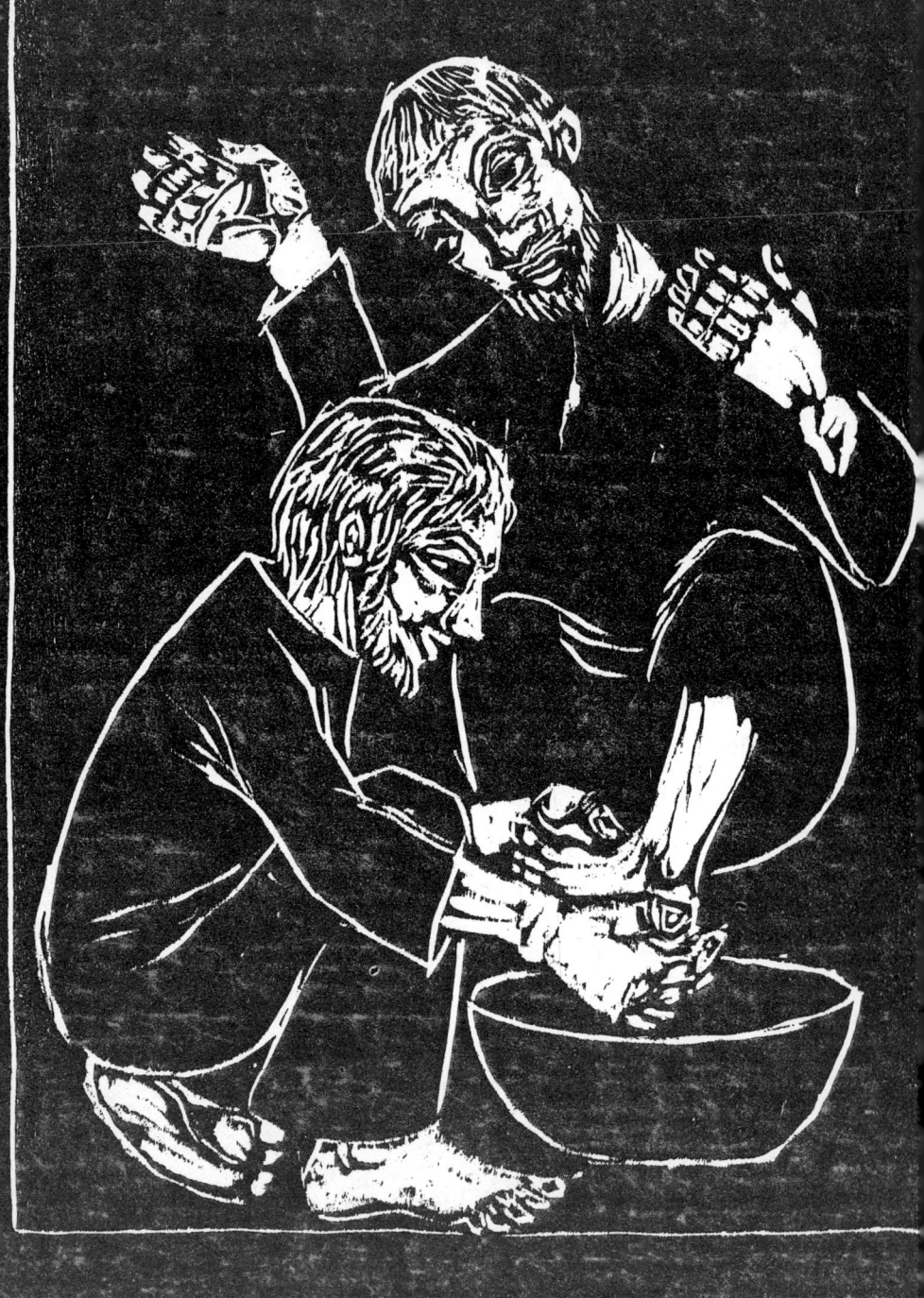

Chapter One

"One Who Serves..."

Throughout the New Testament we read about Jesus, the Son of God, who came to earth as one of us—a human being who was like us in everything except that he never sinned.

It is rather striking that this God-Man so often speaks about the Kingdom of Heaven—his Kingdom—in terms of eating and drinking, of a banquet, of a wedding feast. All these occasions in our world are times when people gather to enjoy each other's company, to be happy and joyous, to "celebrate" some important event.

Our earthly meals, then, are (or should be) a reminder of the heavenly banquet of which Jesus speaks. The Kingdom of Heaven is like a feast that a king gave for his son's wedding (Matthew 22:1–14). Jesus also spoke of the happiness of the person who will be at the feast in the Kingdom of God (Luke 14:15–16), as he related that feast to a man who gave a great banquet and invited a large number of people (Luke 14: 16–24).

It is not without reason then, that Jesus left a memorial of himself at the Last Supper in the form of a meal. At that meal he gives his disciples and us, his followers, his body and blood to be eaten and drunk. At that Last Supper he tells his disciples; "I am among you as the one who serves" (Luke 22:27). At another time, when Jesus was speaking of the end of time, he tells his disciples: ". . . be like servants who await their master's return from a wedding, ready to open immediately when he comes and knocks. Blessed are those servants whom the master finds vigilant on his arrival. Amen, I say to you he will gird himself, have them recline at table and proceed to wait on them." (Luke 12:36–38).

In fact, the community called the Church "is established on the foundation of the service rendered by Jesus. . . . At the time of the Last Supper, Jesus' life was summed up and his death understood as a service, and based on a meal. His attitude of service led Jesus to death, a death that took its meaning from all that had gone before. . . . Jesus lived 'for others,' he would die 'for others,' his enemies and sinners, included."[1]

Jesus himself said that he had "not come to be served but to serve and to give his life as a ransom for many" (Matthew 20:28).

This aspect of Jesus as the servant of others is at the heart of the Gospel according to John, where the evangelist describes how Jesus washed the feet of his disciples during the Last Supper (John 13).

This washing of the feet is Jesus' way of indicating the necessity for mutual help and service in the community which is here established. As Jesus tells Peter: "Unless I wash you, [your feet] you will have no inheritance with me" (John 13:8).

It is true that John does not give any details about the institution of the eucharist, as do other gospel writers. This does not mean that he is unaware of it, nor does he fail to realize its importance. What he is pointing out is that the eucharist is not merely a question of receiving the eucharistic bread and wine, but that those who receive the Lord must live lives of service to their brothers and sisters in the faith, and indeed to all men and women. As Jesus says to his disciples in his last discourse:

"My children, I will be with you only a little while longer . . . I give you a new commandment: love one another. As I have loved you, so you also should love one another" (John 13:33, 34–35).

Jesus is saying that "fraternal love, from its divine source, is the reality which, in the final analysis, is what the eucharist wishes to intensify on earth."[2]

Spirituality Centered in the Eucharist

Special ministers of Holy Communion have been chosen for this ministry because others have already seen in their lives and life-styles a loving readiness to lend a helping hand to those who need it. Like any other person who expends energy on good works, special ministers of Holy Communion need to recharge themselves spiritually. This means that the ministers will find peace, power and new energy the closer they themselves live to their eucharistic Lord. This does not mean that special ministers have to give up all recreation and the pleasures of family and friends. The person who rejects others and pretends to be superior in virtue and piety cannot communicate successfully Jesus' love and life to them.

Jesus gave his life as a pleasing sacrifice to the Father in the Spirit. Christ is present in every eucharist, giving himself to the Father in sacrifice that He might be given to his people as gift in food and drink.

That total self-offering of Jesus to the Father in the Spirit becomes our model in faith and worship. In eucharist we identify with the Christus in the total offering of ourselves to the Father—mind, heart, body, spirit—that we might be a gift of love and peace for others.

The "availability" of Jesus in the eucharist is the pattern for our daily giving of self to the Father and others. In each eucharist we do not worship from afar. We are "close" to Christ in the power and mystery of love, the mystery of Incarnation.

In the holy eucharist the Word of the Father becomes flesh in our midst and dwells among us.

Chapter Two

Becoming Like Christ

We have just seen how Jesus came "not to be served, but to serve." He came for us. He gave his life for us, putting us into a totally new relationship with the Father: ". . . he took the bread, said the blessing, broke it, and gave it to them, saying, "This is my body, which will be given for you; do this in memory of me." And likewise the cup after they had eaten, saying, "This cup is the new covenant in my blood, which will be shed for you." (Luke 22:17–20).

This new covenant relationship with the Father is open to all men and women who want to follow Jesus and live his way of life.

But we cannot live the way Jesus lived in the first century of our era. We have automobiles, electric lights in our houses, all kinds of things the people of Jesus' time did not have. We cannot go back to those days and live the way people did then. So, how can we live Jesus' way of life today?

The answer is by becoming like him more and more every day. We can do this by becoming united with

him in the eucharist. Jesus says:

"I am the bread of life. I am the living bread that came down from heaven; whoever eats this bread will live forever; and the bread that I will give is my flesh for the life of the world." (John 6:48, 51).

As we eat the flesh and drink the blood of Christ in the eucharist we become more and more like him. His life of service, his giving of himself for others, will become our life of service for others.

If we are to be ministers of Christ's body and blood to others, then we must strive to become more and more like him. We should recall and reflect upon the words we heard and the promises we made on the day we were commissioned as ministers of the eucharist.

The presider addresses the candidates: "In this ministry, you must be examples of Christian living in faith and conduct; you must strive to grow in holiness through this sacrament of unity and love. Remember, that, though many, we are one body because we share the one bread and the one cup.

"As ministers of Holy Communion be, therefore, especially observant of the Lord's command to love your neighbor. For, when He gave His body as food to His disciples, He said to them: 'This is my commandment, that you should love one another as I have loved you.'"

After this exhortation, and before the blessing, the presider questions the candidates as to their desire to fulfill their specific ministry within the Church.

"Are you resolved to undertake the Office of giving the Body and Blood of the Lord to your brothers and sisters and so to build up the Church?

"Are you resolved to administer the Holy Eucharist with the utmost care and reverence?"

If we can still answer yes to these questions in all sincerity we must thank God for our faithfulness to him and to the people we serve. But we must also realize that we have to keep in constant touch with the living Christ, if we are to persevere in our good work. We come closest to Jesus and our loving Father in heaven when we take part in the celebration of Mass.

As Catholics we have always known that the Mass is important and that we are required to participate in Mass on Sundays and holy days. But the question is: Could we not participate in Mass with greater love in our hearts for Jesus and the Father and our brothers and sisters in the faith, especially those to whom we will minister the body and blood of Christ?

The first part of the celebration of the eucharist is the service of the Word. Here the written Word of God is proclaimed to the people, a proclamation in which Jesus Christ, the Word of God, speaks to us in the words of the sacred writings.

The service of the Word is replete with examples of holy men and women from the Old Testament who served the Lord with love and self-sacrifice. The prophets call their people back to the Lord when they have forsaken him, as we ourselves often do. The great Fathers in the faith, Abraham, Isaac, Jacob, and the others are models of devotion to duty and of service to their people.

The epistles of the sacred writers, Paul, Peter, James and the others to the early Church preach the Good News of salvation as the people grow in wisdom and understanding of Jesus the Risen Christ. Their trials and temptations are like ours today, and the words of the Apostles are the words of healing. All this is seen in the light of service to God and the brothers and sisters of the growing Church.

In the Gospel reading, we come into closer contact with the Risen Christ. It is he who speaks to us. Here he gives us living examples of his concern for all men and women and shows us how we too can live lives of service to others. It is this Christ who will shortly change the bread and wine into his own body and blood as nourishment for us.

As we treasure all these loving words of Christ and the Apostles and our Fathers in the faith, we prepare to join the Son in offering ourselves to the Father. As the priest prepares the offerings, we may tell Jesus that we too want him to prepare us to be changed into new persons. We are aware of our misdeeds and shortcomings, our plea for patience and quiet but firm love for those we are about to serve as ministers of his body and soul. This is a special moment for those of us who will take the eucharist to the sick and suffering in our community. "Teach us, Lord," we may say, "to be patient with those who are impatient in their suffering; teach us to be like you and love the sick who are difficult to satisfy and are chronic complainers. Teach us to be like you would be if you were right here with us in the sick rooms we are going to visit." We ask Jesus to change us into himself as he changes the bread and wine into his very own self.

The living, Resurrected Jesus Christ who has been present in the celebrant of the Mass, in the congregation gathered in his name and in the readings from Scripture, is now about to become present in another way—a more intense way, a way that makes him come to us as he is in Heaven. This happens at the service of the eucharist. The prayers that accompany Christ's living presence among us ask nothing less than that "we may become one body, one spirit in Christ. May he make us an everlasting gift to you" (Eucharistic Prayer III). And again, we ask the Father to "gather all who share in this bread and wine into the one body of Christ, a living sacrifice of praise" (Eucharistic Prayer IV).

What we are really asking for in these prayers, is that we may not only be like Jesus Christ in patience, kindness, and love for others but that we may, like him, offer ourselves as a living sacrifice.

After communion, we are dismissed to go and serve the Lord and his people.

It is at Mass, then, that the ministers of communion should find solace and strength and the good will to offer both ministry to others and their own lives as a sacrifice of praise to the Father.

Prayer

If we are to be imitators of Christ in our ministry to others, then we need to be people of prayer.

The New Testament records the times when Jesus went apart from his disciples and the crowds to be alone in prayer. Oftentimes, Jesus would go to a mountain to be alone in prayer, sometimes even spending the whole night in prayer (Luke 6:12). St. Luke also records: "but he would withdraw to deserted places to pray" (Luke 5:16).

We all need times like that, times when we can "get away from it all," and pray. Quiet times alone with God in meditation or "prayer of the Heart" nourish and nurture our lives of faith.

As ministers, we are also called to pray not only for

our own needs but also the needs of the communities we serve. Prayer establishes that special intimacy with Christ which allows him to take possession of us. The prayer of the Liturgy of the Hours is an effective way to pray with the Church and as the Church. The daily praying of morning and evening prayer can do much to enrich and enhance one's prayer life, praying in the centuries-old tradition of the Church's prayer. Ministers may also wish to meet occasionally to pray these hours communally. They may even be the spark to set in motion the daily prayer of at least one of the hours in the local parish church.

The private prayer of the Holy Hour before the Blessed Sacrament is a source of great peace, renewal, enlightenment, as well as spiritual and even physical refreshment.

Prayer before the Blessed Sacrament leads us to a greater appreciation for the eucharist as sacrament and sacrifice. The general introduction to the document, "Holy Communion and Worship of the Eucharist Outside Mass" stresses that "in order to encourage devotion to the sacrament of the eucharist correctly, the eucharistic mystery must be considered in all its fullness, both in celebration of Mass and in the worship of the sacrament which is reserved after Mass to extend the grace of the sacrifice" (Article 4).

Of course our love and devotion for the reserved sacrament cannot but help inspire others to the same love and devotion for the eucharist.

Reflection on the Scriptures

Our commitment to ministry needs to be constantly refreshed and renewed. Without being rooted in the Word of God, we can soon go stale and become individuals who are just doing another job. We need to hear that call of the Word of God again and again and allow that call and Word to resound in our hearts, for that call and that Word give us our true identity.

We, as Christians, gather together as a covenant community for worship because we are responding to a call. We sense our identity as the ECCLESIA, as the Church, as the fulfillment of the image of the People of God of the Old Testament, whom God has chosen to be His own people. "Therefore, if you hearken to my voice and keep my covenant, you shall be my special possession, dearer to me than all other people, though all the earth is mine. You shall be to me a kingdom of priests, a holy nation." (Exodus 19:5–6) . . . "a chosen race, a royal priesthood" (1 Peter 2:9).

We are what we are by reason of the powerful and precious Word of God who calls us into existence and sustains us with His all pervasive and supportive grace. The Word of God speaks to us and elicits a response. And we respond to that loving invitation in so far as the soil of our hearts is ready to receive and nurture that seed of the Word of God.

"The seed is the word of God . . . But as for the seed that fell on rich soil, they are the ones who, when they have heard the word, embrace it with a generous and good heart, and, bear fruit through perseverance." (Luke 8:11, 15).

What is true of our attentiveness to the Word of God as a "community of faith" is also true of our openness to the Word as ministers of the community of the faithful.

That Word is a loving invitation spoken to each of us. That Word is a call to be what God would have us be as we penetrate ever more fully into the immense love which Christ has for us.

Special ministers of Holy Communion sometimes feel unworthy of having been chosen for ministry in the Church. Individuals often say: "I really feel humbled by this call to be a special minister of Holy Communion. I feel so unworthy. After all, I'm no saint." The answer to such a situation is to point out that God chooses us frail earthen vessels and calls us to share in His mission and ministry. Conscious of our sinfulness, we realize how much He wants us to be His instruments of healing, peace, and unity among His people, and how much we need His grace to help us do "far more than all we ask or imagine" (Ephesians 3:20). It is His power working in us who believe.

Our response to the Word of God is not a "once for all experience." Our personal response to the call and invitation of God's Word is an every day, around-the-clock experience. We should be so convinced of this need for our communion with the Word of God that we look for every opportunity we can to read the Scriptures, even if for only a few minutes a day.

We can all find little bits of time during the day to open a pocketbook edition of the Bible and read the Word of God on the bus or train, going or coming from work, sitting in the waiting room of a doctor or dentist's office, before going to bed, and so on. There are some people who will rise earlier each morning just to read the Bible in peace and quiet before the children wake up. There are ministers of the eucharist who pack a copy of the New Testament in their lunch boxes and read the Scriptures during their lunch hour.

A minister to be an effective witness to the authentic values of the gospel needs to read the Scriptures daily, as well as pray over them. To give Christ to others, we must know the Christ of the Scriptures.

We must be at home with the Word of God. Only then when we "possess Christ" in ourselves can we offer Christ to others. St. Jerome expressed the power and importance of the Scriptures in the life of the Christian when he said: "Ignorance of the Scriptures is ignorance of Christ."

The Emmaus story (Luke 24:13–35) suggests the role of the Word of God in a minister's spirituality. The disciples on the road to Emmaus came to know the Risen Jesus in the breaking of the bread, as well as the sharing of the Word. "Were not our hearts burning [within us] while he spoke to us on the way and opened the scriptures to us?" (Luke 24:32)

That word must be a constant companion, source of nourishment, reflection and meditation for our tired and weary pilgrim spirits. That word is "living and effective" (Hebrews 4:12), a word which sinks deep into our hearts, falling on the soil of our hearts like rain and snow, and not leaving us until it (he) has born fruit in abundance.

"For just as from the heavens
   the rain and snow come down
And do not return there till they have watered the
   earth, making it fertile and fruitful,
Giving seed to him who sows
   and bread to him who eats,
So shall my word be that goes forth from my mouth;
It shall not return to me void, but shall do my will,
   achieving the end for which I sent it" (Isaiah
   55:10–11).

We are called and sent to be seed and bread; to be fertile and fruitful; to be living Word and loving Sacrament. In Word and in Sacrament we find the One who alone can satisfy the hunger and quench the thirst of every human heart: Jesus, the Bread of Life!

We are privileged and fortunate in our day and age to have available a number of excellent translations of the Scriptures such as the *New American Bible*, the *Jerusalem Bible*, or the *Revised Standard Version*. A visit to your local Christian bookstore will give you an opportunity to compare the various translations of the Scriptures and choose the one best suited to your needs.

Chapter Three

Ongoing Study and Renewal

What does our worship tradition say to us and about us, as ministers of Holy Communion? It says that, first of all, we as ministers, as liturgical servants, are "custodians" of the tradition of the eucharist and all that the Church holds and believes to be true of our eucharistic doctrine. That means we must understand, appreciate, and celebrate devoutly and lovingly the rituals of the Church, especially the eucharist, which incarnate the reality of what we are as God's people and what we as a people believe about the eucharist.

Ministers of Holy Communion need to have a strong group identity, an identity which develops through a well-rounded and solid training and ongoing formation in theology, spirituality, as well as communication and leadership skills.

Ministers need to be understood as more than just "Father's helpers" at Mass. In priestless communities or areas where no ordained minister is present on a regular basis, special ministers of Holy Communion actually serve as prayer-leaders (presiders) for such services as Holy Communion outside Mass, as well as exposition and reposition of the Blessed Sacrament.

In such services, the special minister of Holy Communion acts as a custodian of the eucharist. These pastoral duties demand of the minister a thorough acquaintance with rituals of the Church, as well as the options found in liturgical books, such as the *Lectionary* and the *Sacramentary*.

Perhaps in the past, when this ministry was first introduced, a crash course in "how to" minister the cup and the bread was sufficient. But if ministers and ministries are to be taken seriously, it is necessary for special ministers of Holy Communion to gather for occasional workshops to help improve their skills in pastoral ministry, especially, in "specialized" fields of ministry. Frequent opportunities for "get-togethers" and discussions would be beneficial.

Ministers should attend and want to attend diocesan, regional or intra-parish ministry enrichment programs. Attendance at adult education sessions, especially those dealing with Scripture, liturgy, doctrine, ministry, communication skills, should be on the calendar of yearly or quarterly events for special ministers. Local diocesan or regional seminaries are also willing to open their doors to each Church minister for programs to enrich one's pastoral ministry.

Obviously, all these recommendations should be complemented by one's own regular personal study, research, and reading especially articles pertinent to general or specialized ministry.

Of course, all work and no play makes for a dull ministry, so ministers could form network support groups and take time to share with each other on a social level: a dinner out, field trip, picnic, etc. In all we do as special ministers of Holy Communion, we need to apply the words of the wise adage: "You get out of it what you put into it."

Chapter Four

Attitudes and Demeanor

In the manifold expressions of Christ's presence "we see our God made visible and so are caught up in love of God we cannot see" (Preface of Christmas I, *Sacramentary*).

Reflection upon the mystery of the Incarnation. Will lead one to realize that every minister, ordained and non-ordained, is called to be an instrument of faith, communicating the loving and healing presence of a God who wants so much to be touched and embraced, recognized and appreciated.

Does my ministry make any difference in the community I serve? It can and *it does* to the extent that I allow myself to be so possessed by God that my ministry becomes a reflection of the Incarnate Word. Every minister in living faith and loving service is, indeed, a sacrament of the Word made flesh!

A sacrament? We hear that word and normally identify that word with the Seven Sacraments.

Yet Christ's signs of his love are also revealed in many other ways. Certainly, the Seven Sacraments are pre-eminent in the experience of the Catholic faith. But the term sacrament is not meant to be exclusive; rather it is meant to be inclusive.

Children in parochial school used to memorize the definition of a sacrament that was found in the Baltimore Catechism: "A sacrament is an outward sign instituted by Christ to give grace." But what did all that mean?

The words "outward sign" can well apply to every special minister of Holy Communion. We are neither angelic, nor ethereal. We are flesh and blood; we are persons. Yes, we become "earthly" and visible signs of faith and love which people can touch, feel, and experience.

This is a crucial point for others to understand, especially in cases where the ministry takes place in the home or sickroom. Are we really individuals whom others can touch and feel or do we convey the impression of being untouchable? Do we communicate to those we serve a sense of impersonal formality? Or are we warm and hospitable? As we minister to others, are we afraid to touch their hands or heads? Do our gestures say to another: "Keep your distance"? Does our style of celebration indicate to people that this is just another job to be done, rather than a response to service?

What kind of a "face" do you communicate to others? When a communicant looks at your face, does he or she find a smile, a sense of concern, a personal, warm presence? In human language we call such forms of communication "non-verbal." That is, we say a lot by not speaking.

As ministers we need also to communicate a sense of patience and understanding. That means at times we ministers must "keep our cool" in the face of rebuffs or misunderstanding from those to whom we minister. We have to take in stride an occasional negative comment or off-handed remark, if we are late for a communion call at someone's home or if a patient says to us that he or she does not want to receive communion that day.

Perhaps it might be good for the ministers of communion to stand outside the front doors of the church or in the main vestibule before or after Mass. To do so may help create a sense of warmth between the ministers and the other members of the assembly. If ministers do not greet the people before Mass, perhaps they could do so after the completion of the celebration. This kind of relational experience would also tend to highlight the fact that ministers help create a hospitable environment for worship, as well as to indicate that special ministers do more than distribute Holy Communion. Some may consider this a small point. But when you try to do it, you will be surprised how much the people enjoy the experience.

Coffee hours and socials immediately after Mass are also a good way to bring people of the parish together and build a sense of community. Here, again, the special minister can be an "outward sign," a visible reminder of the servant Christ. If ministers serve food and drink at the eucharistic table of the Lord, would it not also be appropriate and commendable to have them serve coffee, juice, doughnuts and cookies in the parish hall after Mass? People always appreciate congenial hosts and hostesses, as well as pleasant servers at table.

Humility, as a Servant of Christ
Special ministers must never think of their ministry

as a matter of status or privilege. Ministry demands a forgetting of self in the selfless service of the other. Transferred into language of ministry this means that ministers do not consider themselves as "better than others" or somehow even "above" the members of the assembly. Genuine ministry takes place when ministers identify themselves with the assembly and act along with the assembly and for the assembly. That is what the virtue of humility is all about.

I find it hard to believe that in some cases ministers communicate a sense of "doing their own thing." What are ministers saying to the assembly when everyone is singing, but they are not; when the Scriptures are being proclaimed, and they look bored or inattentive; when the homily is delivered and they are yawning? On the positive side, those ministers of the eucharist who immerse themselves in the celebration of Mass, as described in Chapter II, will be an inspiration to others instead of a distraction.

Outward signs communicate so much of who we are and what we know ourselves to be. As ecclesiastical persons and public servants, we need not put on a show for anyone nor should we appear to be show-offs. We are to be authentic signs of Christ's presence and concern by being fully human, caring channels of grace for all those entrusted to our care.

An occasional examination of conscience on the kind of "outward signs" we are should lead us to the point of making adjustments in the way we minister to others in the name of Christ.

The sacraments are effective because they were instituted by Christ to give grace. We, as ministers, are effective insofar as we humbly open ourselves to allow the power and grace of Christ to possess us so that his power and grace may reach out and touch others through our living faith and loving service.

The Minister's Attire

The question of suitable attire for a special minister of Holy Communion can create a lot of heated debate in any parish community.

There are those who would opt for special robes to be worn by the minister of Holy Communion. They feel that the robes add to the beauty and festivity of the celebration of the eucharist. Some would also contend that use of appropriate robes (not formfitting albs or oversized ones that look like potato sacks) resolves the problem of some ministers, who appear at Church for Mass in clothes inappropriate and irreverent to their ministry.

Opponents of such robes claim that the use of robes only appears as a kind of clericalism, and that such dressing up of the ministers makes them seem superior to the other members of the assembly.

There is no simple answer to such a liturgical problem. In certain cases, perhaps, the minister should wear a special robe, such as: when conducting a communion service in the Church or a designated room in a health care facility, or when presiding at exposition or reposition of the Blessed Sacrament.

In places where robes for the special ministers has become a tradition it might not be wise immediately to do away with these garments. Perhaps, if special ministers of Holy Communion wear robes to highlight their ministry, so should the other ministers of the liturgy wear robes; that is, lectors, servers, cantors, psalmists, choir members, and so on. All ministers and ministries should be treated equally.

Some direction in this regard can be found in *Study*

Text I: Holy Communion, published by the Bishops' Committee on the Liturgy. With reference to the garb for special ministers of Holy Communion the text observes: "Special ministers do not wear the liturgical garb of an ordained deacon or priest, but they should be dressed neatly in a way consonant with the dignity of their functional role (e.g., coat and tie for a layman). Local usage should be followed in this matter" (page 15).

As a basic rule of thumb we can state that sloppy clothes or stylish garb are certainly not becoming or appropriate for a special minister of Holy Communion whether at Mass, during a visit to a communicant's home, or conducting a service in a health care facility. The clothes we wear should be a sign of reverence for Christ in the eucharist and Christ present in those to whom we minister.

Sincere Piety and Decorum

Remember the time you were first approached by your pastor, parish priest, or chaplain and asked to become a special minister of Holy Communion? What was your response? Was it: "Who, me? I'm not worthy to become one!"

Perhaps, after completing an initial training program for this ministry, you felt a little more comfortable and knowledgeable as to what were to be the Church's expectations of you in the fulfillment of this pastoral service.

Now, you might well ask yourself:

"How do I celebrate my ministry now? Can I honestly say that I have made some attempt to develop the skills and sensitivities necessary for the fulfillment of my pastoral ministry? How have I renewed myself so that I can continue to be effective in my service to

God's holy people?"

Yes, all ministers must occasionally make not only an examination of conscience of their deeds, but also an examination of consciousness as to the quality of the service they offer God and his people in their specific ministries. We need to reflect again and again on the challenge of a man like Peter, who said: "Be hospitable to one another without complaining. As each one has received a gift, use it to serve one another as good stewards of God's varied grace. " (1 Peter 4:9–11).

All ministries in the Church are essentially ministries of "presence." We, as ministers, communicate the presence of God by our own personal, total and loving presence to our brothers and sisters, fellow members of the Body of Christ. We have the distinct privilege, honor, and responsibility of serving the Body of Christ (the Church), nourishing it with the sacramental Body and Blood of Christ. We assist in a unique way in helping the Word become flesh and blood, to bring hope and strength, healing and joy to so many.

In reality, ours is an awesome responsibility, a noble task, a call to "live in a manner worthy of the call you have received, with all humility and gentleness, with patience, bearing with one another through love, striving to preserve the unity of the spirit through the bond of peace." (Ephesians 4:1–2).

Appreciation of our own accountability before the Lord and his Church should lead us to do all we can to fight any sign of complacency, carelessness, boredom, lethargy, or a perfunctory attitude in the fulfillment of our responsibilities as special ministers of Holy Communion. When a minister begins to distribute the Body of Christ as though he or she were dealing a deck of cards, something is definitely wrong!

One may hope that a fellow minister, a family member, or friend will confront that minister with a gentle correction.

The bishop's words to a priest-candidate in the ritual for the ordination of a presbyter would serve as a good point of personal reflection for all ministers:

"Know what you are doing, and imitate the mystery you celebrate; model your life on the mystery of the Lord's cross."

The Second Vatican Council has continued to exert its impact on the introduction and restoration of liturgical ministries. Pope Paul VI expressed well what the Council Fathers wanted to teach about the Church when he stated: "The Church is not a museum. It is a living organism." And like any living organism the Church will continue to change, not in dogma or doctrine, but in the way which allows the Church to speak the Word of God to the people of each generation.

That sense of change, growth and development will continue to influence every aspect of the Church's life, including worship and ministry. We have cause, then, to continue to reflect on the qualities we need to develop in our pastoral ministry.

Paragraph 49 of *The Constitution on the Sacred Liturgy* states: "Servers, lectors, commentators, and members of the choir all exercise a genuine liturgical ministry. They ought, therefore, to discharge their office with the sincere piety and decorum demanded by so exalted a ministry and rightly expected of them by God's people. Consequently, they must be deeply penetrated with the spirit of the liturgy, each in his/her own measure, and they must be trained to perform their functions in a correct and orderly manner."

We notice that special ministers of Holy Communion are not mentioned in this paragraph. Yet, they should be! When the Constitution was finally promulgated on December 4, 1963, the Council Fathers had not anticipated such a ministry.

Of course, that ministry became a reality ten years later with the appearance of the document, *Immensae Caritatis*, issued January 29, 1973.

Both *Immensae Caritatis* and paragraph 49 of *The Constitution on Sacred Liturgy* offer us a lot of food for thought. They also provide us with a clear course for our ongoing education and renewal as special ministers of Holy Communion.

The former observes:

"The faithful who are special ministers of Holy Communion must be persons whose good qualities of Christian life, faith, and morals recommend them. Let them strive to be worthy of this great office, foster their own devotion to the eucharist, and show an example to the rest of the faithful by their own devotion and reverence toward the most august sacrament of the altar. No one is to be chosen whose appointment the faithful might find disquieting" (*Immensae Caritatis* 1, VI).

Prayerful consideration of this passage should direct us to a serious evaluation of the "good qualities of Christian life, faith and morals" that should be present in a special minister. We should honestly ask ourselves: How does my life and ministry reflect those qualities? Where do I need to improve the quality of my life and Christian witness?

"Foster their own devotion to the eucharist, and show an example to the rest of the faithful by their own devotion and reverence toward the most august sacrament of the altar." Here the role-expectation of the minister is very timely, especially when some people within the Church contend that there is among today's Catholics an apparent loss of the sense of the sacred. It is most significant that the Church in the Rite of Commissioning Special Ministers of Holy Communion rightfully asks each candidate for this ministry: "Are you resolved to administer the Holy Eucharist with the utmost care and reverence?"

We might do well to ask ourselves: What kind of devotion and reverence do I incite in the communicants I serve (at Mass; in the nursing home; at a Communion service)? Is an attitude of reverence and devotion apparent and transparent in the way I actively participate in the liturgy, genuflect, close (not slam) the doors of the tabernacle, walk gracefully across the sanctuary, present the chalice, distribute the Body of Christ, purify the sacred vessels, expose and repose the Blessed Sacrament, handle the pyx when I take Communion outside the Church building?

The Minister's Pastoral Skills

Nathan Mitchell in his scholarly volume, *Cult and Controversy: The Worship of the Eucharist Outside Mass* emphasizes a point about ministers which ought not be neglected:

"Persons chosen to be special ministers should have the qualifications demanded of other liturgical leaders: sensitivity to the pastoral situation, ability to lead others in public prayer, skill in proclaiming the word of God, basic ritual competence."

The author has expressed the development which the service of the special minister of Holy Communion has undergone since the first appearance of such ministers in 1973.

The biblical adage can be most appropriately applied here: "Much will be required of the person entrusted with much, and still more will be demanded of the person entrusted with more." (Luke 12: 48). Added duties and responsibilities of the special minister require that he or she study and develop pastoral skills necessary for the fulfillment of their ministry. But the minister must also weigh the quality and skill he or she uses in the present exercise of the ministry; hence, added duties should not outweigh the present ones.

Take, for example, the simple procedure of distributing Holy Communion. The superb document, "Music in Catholic Worship" exhorts believers to realize and acknowledge that "in true celebration each sign or sacramental action will be invested with the personal and prayerful faith, care, attention, and enthusiasm of those who carry it out" (no. 9).

The manner in which we distribute Holy Communion says a lot about who we are. Within a few seconds of the ritual of presenting the eucharistic bread or cup, a great deal of communication takes place. There is the non-verbal kind: eye contact, a smile, or a warm and inviting expression on the minister's face, the rite of giving and receiving a precious gift. Then, there is the verbal kind: the minister's statement of faith, "the Body (Blood) of Christ" with the responding "Amen" of the communicant.

So simple a set of ritual gestures requires a lot of concentration, skill, practice and expressiveness. When we perform the liturgy well we are literally exhausted. One of the professors in liturgics at the University of Notre Dame used to say that when we come home from the eucharist exhausted and drained, it's probably because we have really celebrated the liturgy!

During this ritual action of distributing the eucharist, as in every pastoral action and responsibility of the special minister of Holy Communion, the minister is a channel of faith, inspiring others to faith by his or her own faith-filled spirit, and leading others to an experience of faith.

The United States Bishops stressed this truth in No. 6 of "Music in Catholic Worship." "Faith grows when it is well expressed in celebration. Good celebrations foster and nourish faith. Poor celebrations may weaken and destroy it."

Special ministers will more and more find themselves exercising the role of a presider. That, too, requires the minister to develop an appreciation for the sense of celebration, an awareness of the structure and mechanics of ritual, and an attractive and gracious style of celebration.

Conducting a Communion service on a Friday afternoon in a senior citizens' residence or nursing home requires more than merely distributing the Holy Eucharist. Certainly the ritual for Communion to the sick by a special minister offers the structure for the service. But the Minister must also bring to the celebration a human sensitivity to the assembly, an ease and facility in celebrating the ritual, a clear and sufficiently audible voice, an awareness of a balance between sound and silence, as well as feeling comfortable with those present for the service, and not getting bent out of shape when something goes wrong!

The same holds true for the celebration of Holy Communion to the sick and handicapped in the home of a parishioner. The ability to put the communicant at ease, to communicate politely and warmly with the person and his or her family, to allow the "other" person to speak and share, to express compassion and concern for the individual—all these skills need to be practiced, and occasionally evaluated by another.

At times a minister may encounter an angry person. Knowledge of the various stages of dying and death, as proposed by Dr. Elizabeth Kubler-Ross,[3] would help a minister to understand that such anger is natural and normal, a stage in the process leading to acceptance of death. No minister should take such anger as directed personally to him or her as a minister.

Lonely persons will tend to open up their hearts to a minister they feel they can trust. Through a series of visits a warm and trusting relationship can develop between the minister and communicant. At times the communicant will feel comfortable and free to unburden his or her worries, concerns or anxiety. You as a minister have to be ready to listen to that person not only with your head, but with your heart. You may even feel at times that you are hearing a person's confession, so much will some people be willing to trust you. And it is always important to remember that what is confided to you must be kept confidential.

A sensitivity to the communicant and his or her feelings at the time of your visit is an important consideration. If on a certain occasion the person seems down and out, take time to be totally present to the person and spend more time with him or her than you usually do.

Be willing and ready to adapt the ritual according to the circumstances of the communicant. If the person is not feeling well that day, perhaps there is need to shorten the ritual celebration.

Ministers also need to be sensitive to persons with

disabilities. Acquaintance with various pastoral situations in which one encounters persons who are disabled is important. An excellent resource in these situations is the audio-visual, *Let Everyone Celebrate*, produced by the Liturgical Commission and Office of Worship of the Diocese of Buffalo. A letter or phone call to a local diocesan office for ministry to persons who are disabled, will allow the minister to obtain information and materials necessary for such ministry.

On occasions where no priest, or deacon is present, a special minister of Holy Communion may be requested to conduct a holy hour, which would include exposition and reposition of the Blessed Sacrament. The minister needs to have facility in incensing the Blessed Sacrament, as well as, at times, even guiding the assembly's singing. In such a case, knowledge of the proper liturgical choreography—where and when to sit; where and when to stand, kneel, or cross the sanctuary, and so on—is essential.

Chapter Five

Extension of the Special Ministry of Holy Communion

With the diminishing number of ordained clergy, special ministers of Holy Communion are more and more undertaking the responsibility to conduct services of the Word, accompanied by the distribution of Holy Communion or exposition and reposition of the Blessed Sacrament. These particular expressions of their ministry are part of the job description for a special minister which the official Church documents not only mention, but even encourage.

When "extraordinary ministers" first appeared in our country shortly after the document *Immensae Caritatis* was issued in January, 1973, we thought of these ministers as those individuals who assisted with the distribution of Holy Communion at Sunday Mass or on other occasions where pastoral necessity demanded their presence.

Since then we have experienced an extension of the special ministry of Holy Communion to the distribution of the eucharist outside Mass (sometimes daily when no priest, or deacon is available); the celebra-

tion of eucharistic exposition and reposition, which involves a liturgy of the Word (see "Holy Communion and Worship of the Eucharist Outside Mass", No. 91); distribution of Holy Communion and Viaticum to the elderly, sick and handicapped persons in their homes; special services in hospitals, skilled-nursing homes, halfway houses, senior citizens' residences, homes for the able-bodied aged, and health care residences for the physically and developmentally disabled adults.

In some parts of the country where priests and deacons are not readily available, special ministers conduct services of the Word with the distribution of ashes on Ash Wednesday, or the blessing of throats, as provided now in the "Rite of Blessing Throats" (see Nos. 6 and 7 of the Introduction of that ritual). Ministers could also conduct Stations of the Cross, Rosary Devotions, days of recollection, Eucharistic Holy Hours, Scripture services and other paraliturgical celebrations.

Ministers have also undertaken specialized kinds of pastoral service such as ministry to the bereaved (conducting wake services, services at the cemetery, follow-up visitations to the family of the deceased) and ministry to prison inmates.

In parochial and institutional settings, special ministers of Holy Communion can offer assistance with liturgy planning teams, implementation of the "Rite of Christian Initiation of Adults," as well as serving the community as catechists and leaders for prayer groups or Scripture study groups.

As we reflect on the increasing variety and types of services exercised by special ministers of Holy Communion, we can see how this ministry has progressed from the view of ministers as simply "waiters and waitresses" at the eucharistic table to multifaceted outreach services to respond with care and concern to the pressing pastoral needs of the community of God's people.

We cannot help but be humble and reverent before the awesome mystery of Incarnation. Admitting our poorness of spirituality and recognizing our human weaknesses and limitations, we acknowledge totally our dependence on the Grace of God "who is able to accomplish far more than all we ask or imagine, by power at work within us." (Ephesians 3: 20).

A principle of classic spirituality teaches us that no person can give what he or she does not have. A minister who lacks faith, cannot offer a dynamic faith to others. A minister who does not know Christ—in the rich biblical sense—cannot lead others to know the Lord. A minister who is not ignited by the Word of God (like the disciples on the road to Emmaus) cannot even so much as emit a spark of faith and love to another. Our hearts must burn within us as the Lord continues to meet us on the road of life and speaks to us through the Scriptures.

Bibliography

A. Documentation

Bishops' Committee on the Liturgy. "Music in Catholic Worship", Washington, D.C.: USCC Publications Service. 1983

International Committee on English in the Liturgy, Inc. *Holy Communion and Worship of the Eucharist Outside Mass.* Washington, D.C., 1974.

B. Books

Belford, William J., Special Ministers of the Eucharist. Pueblo Publishing, New York, 1984.

Champlin, Msgr. Joseph - *An Important Office of Immense Love*, Paulist Press - Ramsey, N.J. 1980

Federation of Diocesan Liturgical Commissions. *The Mystery of Faith: A Study of the Structural Elements of the Order of Mass.* Washington, D.C. 1980.

Hovda, Robert. *Strong, Loving, and Wise: Presiding in Liturgy.* Liturgical Press, Collegeville, Minnesota. 5th Printing, 1980.

Kern, Rev. Walter - *Pastoral Ministry with Disabled Persons.* Alba House, Staten Island, N.Y. 1985

The Liturgical Conference - *Touchstones for Liturgical Ministers.* The Liturgical Conference and the Federation of Diocesan Liturgical Commissions. Washington, D.C. 1978.

Mitchell, Nathan. *Cult and Controversy: The Worship of the Eucharist Outside Mass.* Pueblo Publishing Co., New York. 1982

C. *Audio Visuals*

Buffalo, Diocese of. "Let Everyone Celebrate," Meta-Media, Buffalo, N.Y. 1986. Slides/Filmstrip on Ministry to Persons Who Are Sick or Disabled.

Champlin, Msgr. Joseph. "Together by your Side. A Program on How to Comfort the Sick, the Dying and the Bereaved," Ave Maria Press, Notre Dame, Indiana. 1980

O'Dea, Barbara. "Bread and Cup," National Catholic Reporter Cassettes. Kansas City, Missouri. Cassettes.

Paulist Press. "Be What You Celebrate," Ramsay, N.J. 1982.

Thompson - O'Shea Associates. "Let Us Give Thanks: A History of God's People at Mass." Joliet, Illinois 1968.

Twenty-Third Publications. "Lay Ministries Training Program." Mystic, Connecticut.